ASTERIX THE GAUL

TEXT BY GOSCINNY

DRAWINGS BY UDERZO

TRANSLATED BY ANTHEA BELL AND DEREK HOCKRIDGE

HODDER DARGAUD
LONDON SYDNEY AUCKLAND

GAUL
(ROMAN CONQUEST)
50 B.C.

The year is 50BC. Gaul is entirely occupied by the Romans. Well, not entirely... One small village of indomitable Gauls still holds out against the invaders. And life is not easy for the Roman legionaries who garrison the fortified camps of Totorum, Aquarium, Laudanum and Compendium...

a few of the Gauls

Asterix, the hero of these adventures. A shrewd, cunning little warrior; all perilous missions are immediately entrusted to him. Asterix gets his superhuman strength from the magic potion brewed by the druid Getafix…

Obelix, Asterix's inseparable friend. A menhir delivery-man by trade; addicted to wild boar. Obelix is always ready to drop everything and go off on a new adventure with Asterix – so long as there's wild boar to eat, and plenty of fighting.

Getafix, the venerable village druid. Gathers mistletoe and brews magic potions. His speciality is the potion which gives the drinker superhuman strength. But Getafix also has other recipes up his sleeve…

Cacofonix, the bard. Opinion is divided as to his musical gifts. Cacofonix thinks he's a genius. Everyone else thinks he's unspeakable. But so long as he doesn't speak, let alone sing, everybody likes him…

Finally, Vitalstatistix, the chief of the tribe. Majestic, brave and hot-tempered, the old warrior is respected by his men and feared by his enemies. Vitalstatistix himself has only one fear; he is afraid the sky may fall on his head tomorrow. But as he always says, 'Tomorrow never comes.'

IN THE YEAR 50 BC, AFTER A LONG STRUGGLE, THE ANCIENT GAULS HAD BEEN CONQUERED BY THE ROMANS.....

CHIEFS LIKE VERCINGETORIX HAD TO LAY THEIR ARMS AT CAESAR'S FEET.....

OUCH!

CLANG!

PEACE REIGNS, DISTURBED ONLY BY OCCASIONAL ATTACKS BY THE GERMANS, SPEEDILY REPULSED.....

So! But ve komm back!

Gut! Ve go!

ALL GAUL IS OCCUPIED.....

ALL? NO-ONE VILLAGE STILL HOLDS OUT STUBBORNLY AGAINST THE INVADERS. ONE SMALL VILLAGE SURROUNDED BY FORTIFIED ROMAN CAMPS.....

ALL EFFORTS TO SUBDUE THESE PROUD GAULS HAVE FAILED, AND CAESAR ASKS HIMSELF.....

QUID?

AND NOW WE MEET OUR HERO, THE WARRIOR ASTERIX, JUST OFF HUNTING AS USUAL

BACK SOON, ASTERIX?

I'LL BE BACK FOR DINNER, OBELIX

HERE HE COMES!

WE'LL GET HIM

IPSO FACTO!

SIC!

BIFF! OW! BANG! OUCH!

ACCIDENCE WILL HAPPEN.....

VAE VICTO VAE VICTIS!

WE DECLINE!

HERE IS THE POTION THAT MAKES THE DRINKER INVINCIBLE! IT INCREASES HIS STRENGTH TENFOLD – FOR A LIMITED PERIOD OF TIME

WHAT'S THE RECIPE, O DRUID?

THE ORIGIN OF THIS RECIPE IS LOST IN THE MISTS OF TIME. IT IS HANDED DOWN FROM DRUID TO DRUID BY WORD OF MOUTH....

ALL I CAN REVEAL IS THAT THERE'S MISTLETOE AND LOBSTER IN IT....

THE LOBSTER IS OPTIONAL, BUT IT IMPROVES THE FLAVOUR!

SPLOSH!

CAN I HAVE SOME?

NO, OBELIX, YOU CAN NOT AND WELL YOU KNOW IT!

YOU FELL INTO THE CAULDRON WHEN YOU WERE A BABY, AND IT HAD A PERMANENT EFFECT ON YOU. IT WOULD BE DANGEROUS FOR YOU TO DRINK ANY MORE!

THANKS, O DRUID!

IT'S NOT FAIR, BY BELENOS!

OW! OW! OW!

I'VE TOLD YOU BEFORE NOT TO SHAKE HANDS WITH ME WHEN YOU'VE JUST HAD YOUR POTION

HE'S RIGHT, I DON'T KNOW MY OWN STRENGTH!

WAIT A MINUTE!

HM?

SSH!

BUT...

I CAN HEAR FOOTSTEPS—CHAINS CLANKING—SOMEONE WAILING!

!

LET'S HIDE AT THE TOP OF THIS TREE! WE MAY SOON BE LOOSENING UP OUR MUSCLES!

BY ALL THE GODS, I SHOULD HAVE STAYED AT HOME! I NEVER OUGHT TO HAVE JOINED CAESAR'S LEGIONS IN SEARCH OF FAME AND FORTUNE! MY SKIN'S NOT WORTH A SESTERTIUS AND I'LL NEVER EAT TAPIOCA (I) LIKE MOTHER MADE AGAIN!

(I) SPAGHETTI WAS NOT IMPORTED FROM CHINA BY MARCO POLO UNTIL MUCH LATER.

WILL YOU SHUT UP, CALIGULA MINUS! AFTER ALL, WHEN THE HORDES OF GAULS ATTACK US YOU'RE THE ONLY ONE THEY'LL SPARE!

SURE ENOUGH, THERE ARE THE HORDES..

ROMANS, WITH A GAUL AS PRISONER!

WE'LL RESCUE HIM!

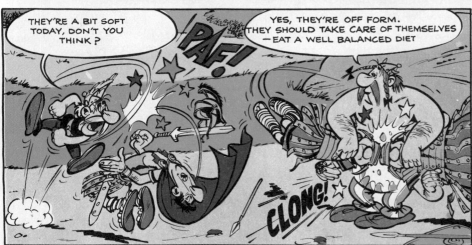

MARCUS GINANTONICUS AND HIS HEROIC DETACHMENT RETURN TO COMPENDIUM....

TCHIC: BLDZRRZLM MDLXVIIM NIZDRC

THE GAULS CAME AND SAW AND CONQUERED CALIGULA MINUS!

A GREAT VICTORY FOR US!

LET'S HOPE CALIGULA MINUS GETS BACK IN ONE PIECE TO TELL US WHAT HE'S SEEN!

HE'D BETTER! IF NOT I'LL HAVE SOMETHING TO SAY TO HIS ROMAN REMAINS!

ALEA JACTA EST!

PARDON?

MEANWHILE....

THIS IS OUR VILLAGE, CALIGULIMINIX. YOU'LL BE SAFE HERE! IT'S FULL OF GAULS!

THAT'S A GREAT COMFORT

ASTERIX AND OBELIX ARE BACK!

THEY'VE GOT SOMETHING WITH THEM!

SOMETHING VERY PECULIAR, BY BELENOS!

COME AND MEET OUR CHIEF, VITALSTATISTIX

BUT— BUT THEY'RE ALL ARMED!

YES, WE HAVE TO BE PREPARED TO FIGHT THE ROMANS AT THE DROP OF A HELMET

A WISE PRECAUTION!

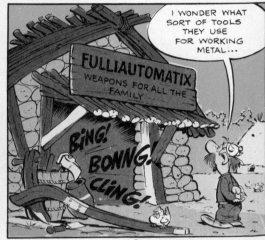

WE'LL TORTURE THE DRUID. THEN HE'LL TALK ALL RIGHT!

WELL, ARE YOU TALKING?

NO, YOU ARE!

MUCH LATER...

LOOK HERE, DRUID, THIS ISN'T FUNNY! WE'VE BEEN TORTURING YOU FOR HOURS, AND IT DOESN'T EVEN SEEM TO HURT. THIS WON'T HELP YOU!

OH YES, IT WILL; IT'LL HELP TO PASS THE TIME

DRUID, IF YOU TALK I CAN MAKE YOU RICH AND POWERFUL!

NO!

YOU'LL HAVE SESTERTII! LOADS OF SESTERTII!

NO!

IS THIS TORTURE GOING ON MUCH LONGER? I'VE GOT BETTER THINGS TO DO!

THIS DRUID'S MAGIC POWERS ARE TOO MUCH FOR ME — AND IS HE PIGHEADED!

MEANWHILE...

WHAT'S THE MATTER, ASTERIX? YOU LOOK WORRIED

OUR DRUID WENT TO THE FOREST TO PICK MISTLETOE, AND HE HASN'T COME BACK...

I'M GOING TO LOOK FOR HIM!

WATCH OUT, ASTERIX! IT'S A LONG TIME SINCE YOU HAD ANY POTION!

HUH! I'M RELYING ON MY CUNNING TO FIND THE DRUID!

24

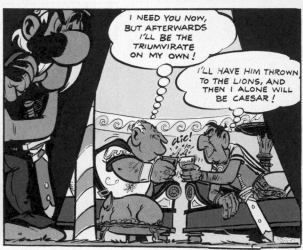

MOST INTERESTING, BUT IT TELLS ME NOTHING OF GETAFIX'S WHEREABOUTS!

HE MUST BE IN THAT HEAVILY GUARDED TENT...

THE BOLD APPROACH!

DO YOU MIND? I'VE JUST COME TO RESCUE GETAFIX THE DRUID. HE'S A FRIEND OF MINE

?!?!?!

THANKS!

DON'T LET HIM OUT! HE'S ONE OF THOSE INVINCIBLE GAULS... MAGIC POTION FAIRLY OOZING OUT OF HIS EARS! I'M GOING FOR REINFORCEMENTS!

V...VERY WELL! BUT DON'T BE LONG, O CAIUS FLEBITUS!

AND INSIDE THE TENT...

ASTERIX!

ALL WELL?

BY BELISAMA, ASTERIX! WHAT MADNESS TO VENTURE RIGHT INTO THE JAWS OF THE ROMAN WOLF!

THE ROMANS CAN'T DO A THING AGAINST MY MAGIC POWERS!

EXACTLY! WE'LL HAVE SOME FUN WITH THEM! I'VE GOT A FEW IDEAS!

SIR! SIR!

30

WELL, IF YOU DON'T NEED ME ANY MORE I'LL BE OFF...

GEE UP!

WAIT A MINUTE! IF I GOT IT RIGHT, I'M VERY STRONG NOW!

THIS IS GREAT! NOW I CAN SELL MY OXEN AND PULL THE CART MYSELF!

THAT POTION...

... CERTAINLY DOES HAVE...

... MAGIC POWERS!

AND AT COMPENDIUM...

GLUG GLUG GLUG GLUG!

COME ON, EVERYONE! LET'S ALL DRINK THE MAGIC POTION!

THIS 𝝅𝟞✳✻ CAULDRON WHERE THEY BREWED THAT ◇✳〰〜'◎⚡ POTION!

BANG!

SLAP! SLAP! SLAP!

THREE THOUSAND, FOUR HUNDRED AND FIFTY...

?

WHAT DID YOU SAY?

WE'VE INVENTED A NEW GAME. EVERY TIME WE SEE A MAN WITH A BEARD WE SCORE FIFTEEN. THE ONE WITH THE HIGHEST SCORE WINS! (1)

(1) A GAME STILL PLAYED TODAY IN CERTAIN PARTS OF WESTERN EUROPE

YOU'RE MAKING FUN OF ME, GAUL. BUT I HAVE TO TALK TO YOU!

TALK AWAY, THEN! LET'S NOT SPLIT ANY HAIRS

YELP! YELP! YELP!

WILL YOU SHUT UP ABOUT HAIR!!!

POF! POF! POF!

WELL, IF YOU WILL BEARD US IN OUR OWN TENT...

NO, DON'T GO!

HI! HI!

ALL RIGHT, KEEP YOUR HAIR ON!

HA! HA! HO! HO!

OR THIS TALK WILL BRISTLE WITH DIFFICULTIES. GO ON!

HA! HA! STOP! STOP! HA! HA! HA! HA!

THUMP! THUMP! THUMP!

AHA! SO THESE ARE THE TERRIBLE GAULS!

TELL ME WHAT THIS IS ALL ABOUT...

CRISMUS BONUS WAS EXTREMELY EAGER TO GET HOLD OF THE RECIPE FOR A MAGIC POTION WHICH WOULD HAVE MADE HIM INVINCIBLE, REMOVING ALL OBSTACLES BETWEEN HIMSELF AND THE IMPERIAL THRONE...

WELL, WELL!

I CAN EXPLAIN EVERYTHING!

DON'T BOTHER! GO AND SHAVE. THEN YOU AND YOUR MEN WILL SET OFF FOR OUTER MONGOLIA. I HEAR THERE'S A BARBARIAN REBELLION THERE...

AS FOR YOU, IN EXCHANGE FOR THE SERVICE YOU HAVE RENDERED ME, I GRANT YOU YOUR FREEDOM...

BUT THIS IS ONLY A TRUCE, GAUL. WE SHALL MEET AGAIN!

I'M COUNTING ON IT, O JULIUS!

SOON AFTERWARDS...

BY TOUTATIS, HERE THEY ARE!

AND ALL NIGHT LONG BY THE LIGHT OF THE MOON, UNDER A STARRY SKY, THE GAULS FEAST THEIR HEROES, VICTORIOUS OVER THEIR ENEMIES THANKS TO MAGIC, THE PROTECTION OF THE GODS, AND LOW CUNNING...

I COULD EAT ANOTHER BOAR...

ASTERIX AND THE GOTHS

TEXT BY GOSCINNY

DRAWINGS BY UDERZO

TRANSLATED BY ANTHEA BELL AND DEREK HOCKRIDGE

GAULISH VILLAGE

COMPENDIUM

AQUARIUM

LAUDANUM

TOTORUM

ARMORICA

BELGICA

LUTETIA

SPQR

GAUL
(ROMAN CONQUEST)
50 B.C.

CELTICA

PROVINCIA

AQUITANIA

The year is 50 BC. Gaul is entirely occupied by the Romans. Well, not entirely... One small village of indomitable Gauls still holds out against the invaders. And life is not easy for the Roman legionaries who garrison the fortified camps of Totorum, Aquarium, Laudanum and Compendium...

a few of the Gauls

Asterix, the hero of these adventures. A shrewd, cunning little warrior; all perilous missions are immediately entrusted to him. Asterix gets his superhuman strength from the magic potion brewed by the druid Getafix...

Obelix, Asterix's inseparable friend. A menhir delivery-man by trade; addicted to wild boar. Obelix is always ready to drop everything and go off on a new adventure with Asterix – so long as there's wild boar to eat, and plenty of fighting.

Getafix, the venerable village druid. Gathers mistletoe and brews magic potions. His speciality is the potion which gives the drinker superhuman strength. But Getafix also has other recipes up his sleeve...

Cacofonix, the bard. Opinion is divided as to his musical gifts. Cacofonix thinks he's a genius. Everyone else thinks he's un-speakable. But so long as he doesn't speak, let alone sing, everybody likes him...

Finally, Vitalstatistix, the chief of the tribe. Majestic, brave and hot-tempered, the old warrior is respected by his men and feared by his enemies. Vitalstatistix himself has only one fear; he is afraid the sky may fall on his head tomorrow. But as he always says, 'Tomorrow never comes.'

5

WHILE THESE SERIOUS FRONTIER INCIDENTS ARE TAKING PLACE, OUR FRIENDS ARE ON THEIR WAY TO THE FOREST OF THE CARNUTES...

WE'LL SOON BE THERE. YOU SEE, IT WAS QUITE AN UNEVENTFUL JOURNEY!

BETTER SAFE THAN SORRY...

I'M A BIT PECKISH...

OH! WHAT A PLEASANT SURPRISE!

A WILD BOAR?!

FRIENDS, LET ME INTRODUCE YOU TO MY OLD FRIEND AND COLLEAGUE, THE BRITISH DRUID VALUADDETAX!

OH, I SAY! DELIGHTED, I'M SURE!

COME ALONG, VALUADDETAX! I'M GOING TO AMAZE YOU WITH MY DRUIDICAL PROWESS!

WAIT TILL YOU SEE MINE, OLD BOY!

HALT! WHO GOES THERE?

A ROMAN PATROL!

SHALL WE GET THEM?

NO, NO, OBELIX. WHILE THE CONFERENCE IS ON THERE'S A TRUCE WITH THE ROMANS.

LET US PASS, DECURION. WE ARE DRUIDS GOING TO THE FOREST OF THE CARNUTES.

THAT'S YOUR STORY. JUST PROVE IT!

7

THE FOREST OF THE CARNUTES IS SWARMING WITH DRUIDS IN MERRY MOOD, ALL DELIGHTED TO SEE EACH OTHER AGAIN...

EVERY OAK TREE IS FULL OF DRUIDS HARD AT WORK CUTTING MISTLETOE WITH THEIR SICKLES...

SNIP!

SNIP!

SNIP!

SWISH!

OOOOUCH! THAT'S MY FINGER!

THEY TALK SHOP, THEY DISCUSS SPELLS...

YES, MY DEAR FELLOW, I PICKED UP THIS SICKLE IN A LITTLE SHOP IN DARIORIGUM! LOOK, IT'S GOT A SAFETY-CATCH.

SO THEN, OLD MAN, HEY PRESTO! I TURNED HIM INTO A MENHIR!

THEY EVEN INDULGE IN JOKES AND PUNS... IN SHORT, THEY ARE HAVING A GOOD TIME.

THIS FOOD'S A BIT SICKLE-Y!

PASS ME THE CELT!

IT MUST BE HIS GAUL BLADDER!

MENHIR A TRUE WORD IS SPOKEN IN JEST!

THEN, AFTER THE GREAT BANQUET...

SILENCE, BROTHERS, SILENCE!

CLANG! CLANG!

CLANG!

BROTHER DRUIDS, THE TIME HAS COME FOR US TO BEGIN OUR GREAT CONTEST TO EVALUATE NEW METHODS AND ELECT THE DRUID OF THE YEAR...

AND WHILE THE DRUIDS PREPARE THEIR MAGIC POTIONS...

...GREEDY EYES ARE WATCHING THEM...

Now comes the interesting part!

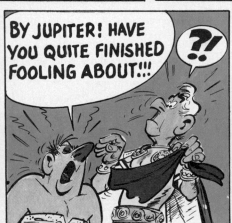

23

ASTERIX AND OBELIX ARE NOT THE ONLY ONES WITH ESCAPE IN MIND, FOR IN ANOTHER PART OF THE TOWN...

I'LL GO TO GAUL. WITH MY KNOWLEDGE OF MODERN LANGUAGES I'LL BE ABLE TO GET A JOB THERE...

Halt! Who goes there?

THE PATROL!

Well, if it isn't Rhetoric the interpreter! And where might you be off to at this time of night?

Well, I...er...the fact is...well, it was like this, you see...

No, I don't! It's the guardroom for you! You can explain yourself tomorrow!

No, No! You're making a big mistake! I've got friends in high places!!!

I'M DONE FOR! THE CHIEF WILL NEVER FORGIVE ME FOR DECEIVING HIM ABOUT WHAT THAT PIG-HEADED DRUID SAID...

MEANWHILE...

GOT IT? NO FIGHTING, AND NO TALKING TO ANY GOTHS.

RIGHT!

!

EEEK! THATS TORN IT!

Hullo, hullo, hullo! Who have we here? You're for the guardroom too!

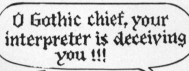

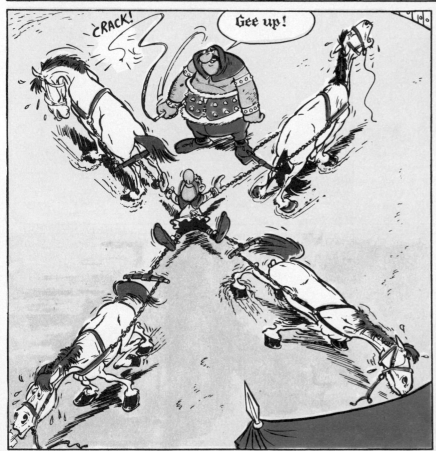

ASTERIX, GETAFIX AND OBELIX MAKE THEIR WAY BACK TO THE DUNGEON FOR A WORD WITH METRIC...

Metric, would you like to get your revenge on Rhetoric and return to power?

?

HE SAYS YES!

I GOT THE GENERAL IDEA!

Have a swig of this magic potion... then you'll be as strong as Rhetoric. The way you use your strength is up to you...

!

GLUG! GLUG!

CLINNNK!

HE'S GOT A FREE HAND NOW!

CRAAAAASH!

Here we go again! They ought to replace that door by a curtain!

Raise the alarm! The prisoner's escaping !!!

So what?

POC!

HE'S GOT A FREE HAND! HA!HA!HA! THATS A GOOD ONE, THAT IS! I'VE ONLY JUST GOT IT. HO!HO!HO!

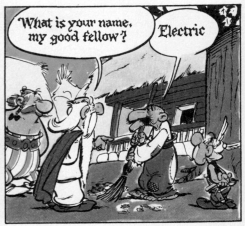

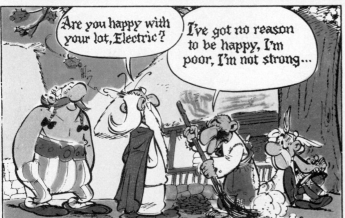

< footer>

Metric

Rhetoric

THE ASTERIXIAN WARS
A Tangled Web . . .

The ruse employed by Asterix, Getafix and Obelix succeeded beyond their wildest dreams. After drinking the druid's magic potion, the Goths fought each other tooth and nail. Here is a brief summary to help you follow the history of these famous wars.

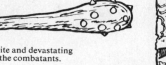

The favourite and devastating weapon of the combatants.

Diagram indicating the course of events.

The first victory is won outright by Rhetoric, who, having surprised Metric by an outflanking movement, lets him have it – bonk! – and inflicts a crushing defeat on him. This defeat, however, is only temporary . . .

Rhetoric has no time to celebrate his victory, for, having completed his outflanking movement, he is taken in the rear by his own ally, Lyric. Lyric instantly proclaims himself supreme chief of all the Goths, much to the amusement of the other chiefs . . . .

Who turn out to be right, for Lyric's brother-in-law Satiric lays an ambush for him, pretending to invite him to a family reunion and Lyric falls into the trap. It was upon this occasion that the proposition that blood is thicker than water was first put to the test . . .

Rhetoric goes after Lyric, with the avowed intention of "bashing him up" (archaic), but his rearguard is surprised by Metric's vanguard. Bonk! This manoeuvre is known as the Metric System.

General Electric manages to surprise Euphoric meditating on the conduct of his next few campaigns. Euphoric's morale is distinctly lowered, but he has the last word, with his famous remark, "I'll short-circuit him yet"

While Electric proclaims himself supreme chief of the Goths, to the amusement of all and sundry, it is the turn of Metric's rearguard to be surprised by Rhetoric's vanguard. Bonk! "This is bad for my system," is the comment of the exasperated Metric.

In fact, it is so bad for his system that he allows himself to be surprised by Euphoric. The battle is short and sharp. Euphoric, a wily politician, instantly proclaims himself supreme chief of the Goths. The other supreme chiefs are in fits . . .

Euphoric, much annoyed, sets up camp and decides to sulk. He is surprised by Eccentric, who in his turn is attacked by Lyric, subsequently to be defeated by Electric. Electric is destined to be betrayed by Satiric, who will be beaten by Rhetoric.

Going round a corner, Rhetoric's vanguard bumps into Metric's vanguard. Bonk! Bonk! This battle is famous in the Asterixian wars as the "Battle of the Two Losers" And so the war goes on . . .

MEANWHILE, OUR THREE FRIENDS ARE APPROACHING THE FRONTIER OF GAUL, WITH THEIR MINDS AT REST . . .

ASTERIX
THE GLADIATOR

TEXT BY GOSCINNY

DRAWINGS BY UDERZO

TRANSLATED BY ANTHEA BELL AND DEREK HOCKRIDGE

GAULISH VILLAGE

COMPENDIUM

LAUDANUM

AQUARIUM

TOTORUM

ARMORICA

BELGICA

LUTETIA

SPQR

GAUL
(ROMAN CONQUEST)
50 B.C.

CELTICA

PROVINCIA

AQUITANIA

The year is 50 BC. Gaul is entirely occupied by the Romans.
Well, not entirely... One small village of indomitable Gauls still
holds out against the invaders. And life is not easy for the
Roman legionaries who garrison the fortified camps of
Totorum, Aquarium, Laudanum and Compendium...

a few of the Gauls

Asterix, the hero of these adventures. A shrewd, cunning little warrior; all perilous missions are immediately entrusted to him. Asterix gets his superhuman strength from the magic potion brewed by the druid Getafix...

Obelix, Asterix's inseparable friend. A menhir delivery-man by trade; addicted to wild boar. Obelix is always ready to drop everything and go off on a new adventure with Asterix — so long as there's wild boar to eat, and plenty of fighting.

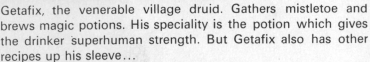

Getafix, the venerable village druid. Gathers mistletoe and brews magic potions. His speciality is the potion which gives the drinker superhuman strength. But Getafix also has other recipes up his sleeve...

Cacofonix, the bard. Opinion is divided as to his musical gifts. Cacofonix thinks he's a genius. Everyone else thinks he's unspeakable. But so long as he doesn't speak, let alone sing, everybody likes him...

Finally, Vitalstatistix, the chief of the tribe. Majestic, brave and hot-tempered, the old warrior is respected by his men and feared by his enemies. Vitalstatistix himself has only one fear; he is afraid the sky may fall on his head tomorrow. But as he always says, 'Tomorrow never comes.'

6

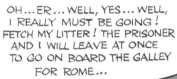

YOU HAVE SAVED WHAT IS DEAREST TO OUR HEARTS — OUR CARGO! NOW WE'RE BOSOM FRIENDS!

I ORIGINALLY INTENDED TO SELL YOU AS SLAVES WHEN WE CALLED AT THE NEXT PORT. BUT NOW I'LL TAKE YOU TO ROME AS AGREED

YOU CERTAINLY DO HAVE BUSINESS ACUMEN!

WHAT CAN YOU EXPECT? AS I WAS SAYING TO MY PARTNERS, WE'RE ALL IN THE SAME BOAT, AND WE MUSTN'T REST ON OUR OARS IF OUR OVERHEADS ARE NOT TO MAKE US GO UNDER!

MEANWHILE, IN ROME...

AVE, CAESAR!

AVE, ODIUS ASPARAGUS, PREFECT OF GAUL

HERE'S MY PRESENT, O CAESAR! A GAULISH BARD FROM THE TRIBE OF INDOMITABLE GAULS IN THE COMPENDIUM AREA

I'VE BEEN BROUGHT HERE AS A SOUVENIR... JUST AS IF I WAS A VULGAR PAINTED SHELL!

A BARD? HOW INTERESTING!

YOU CAN WAIT TILL THE COWS COME HOME BEFORE I'LL SING FOR YOU... AND YOU DON'T KNOW WHAT YOU'RE MISSING!

THANKS FOR THIS ORIGINAL LITTLE PRESENT, PREFECT. YOU MAY GO!

SEND FOR CAIUS FATUOUS, THE LANISTA*

SNAP!

* TRAINER OF THE GLADIATORS

CAIUS FATUOUS, CAN YOU MAKE A GLADIATOR OF THIS BARD?

DEAR ME, NO, O CAESAR! HE'S TOO WEAK ... NOT ENOUGH MEAT ON HIM

IF I WASN'T RESTRAINING MYSELF...

VERY WELL THEN, THROW HIM TO THE LIONS AT THE NEXT GAMES. TAKE HIM AWAY!

WE'RE NEARING THE END OF OUR VOYAGE. ROME IS A FEW HOURS' WALK FROM THE PLACE WHERE WE'RE GOING TO LAND...

WE'LL BE STAYING HERE FOR A WHILE TO BUY AND SELL GOODS. IF YOU FINISH YOUR BUSINESS IN TIME WE'LL TAKE YOU BACK TO GAUL...

THANKS, EKONOMI-KRISIS!

HOIST THE FLAG!

SALE FINAL CLEARANCE

JUST LOOK AT THIS, OBELIX! IF THE ROADS ARE SO WIDE AND STRAIGHT HERE, WHAT MUST IT BE LIKE IN ROME?

DANGER SLIPPERY FLAGSTONES

WE'RE THERE!

VIA APPIA
ROMA

?!?

HOW ABOUT THAT HELMET GAME AGAIN? WE COULD HAVE A LOVELY FIGHT WITH ALL THESE ROMANS!

WE MUST START MAKING INQUIRIES... AND I THINK I SEE WHAT WE NEED!

14

18

19

22

YES, I DID HEAR ABOUT THE BARD THAT THE PREFECT OF GAUL GAVE CAESAR AS A PRESENT...

IT SEEMS THAT THIS BARD IS TO BE THROWN TO THE LIONS AT THE NEXT GAMES IN THE CIRCUS MAXIMUS, IN A FEW DAYS' TIME...

!!

WE'LL RESCUE HIM!

YOU CAN'T. THE BARD'S BEEN SHUT UP IN A CELL IN THE CIRCUS... AND IT'S A MAXIMUM SECURITY CIRCUS!

BUT THERE'S WORSE TO COME. THAT'S WHY I WARNED YOU TO BE CAREFUL. YOU MUST BE INDOMITABLE GAULS LIKE THE BARD! YOU MUST FLEE FROM ROME!

CAIUS FATUOUS, WHO TRAINS THE GLADIATORS, IS LOOKING FOR MEN FOR THE GAMES... AND INDOMITABLE GAULS ARE IN GREAT DEMAND!

WE WILL RESCUE OUR BARD!

YOU ACT THE FINE LADY AND YOU CAN'T EVEN AFFORD A SLAVE TO DO THE HOUSEWORK!

SO I AM A FINE LADY! SO YOU KNOW WHAT THE FINE LADY HAS TO SAY TO YOU?

BY JUNO, IF YOU DON'T SHUT UP I'M CALLING THE WATCH!

THESE ROMANS ARE CRAZY!

THERE THEY ARE!

WE'RE BEING ATTACKED!

GOODY!

LOOK, ASTERIX! I'VE THOUGHT OF SOMETHING NEW! LOOK, I DON'T EVEN TOUCH THEM, I SHAKE THEM! IT LASTS LONGER THAT WAY!

ALL RIGHT, OBELIX. PUT HIM DOWN NOW!

WILL YOU BE QUIET OUT THERE IN THE ROAD! WE CAN'T HEAR OURSELVES SHOUT IN HERE!

19

26

27

31

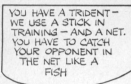

TIME PASSES BY, AND THE GLADIATORS ARE PUTTING ON WEIGHT...

MY FIRST IS A HUNDRED, MY SECOND IS A SIGN OF THE ZODIAC, MY THIRD IS A HIBERNIAN, MY FOURTH IS THE EGYPTIAN GOD OF THE SUN AND JULIUS CAESAR LOVES MY WHOLE! WHO AM I?

WHILE CAIUS FATUOUS IS LOSING IT...

THERE THEY GO AGAIN! PLAYING IDIOTIC GAMES INSTEAD OF TRAINING! A FINE CIRCUS THIS IS GOING TO BE!

IT'S C, LEO, PAT, RA... CLEOPATRA!

THAT WAS A DIFFICULT ONE THAT WAS!

THE GAMES ARE FIXED FOR TOMORROW. THIS WILL BE YOUR LAST NIGHT IN THE CIRCUS, YOU USELESS LOT!

WE DON'T REALLY WANT TO FIGHT ANY MORE, ASTERIX

DON'T WORRY! I PROMISE YOU WON'T HAVE TO RISK YOUR LIVES IN THE ARENA!

AND A VERY RELAXED GROUP OF GLADIATORS ARRIVES AT THE CIRCUS...

HA, HA! HO, HO!

STOP PUSHING, WILL YOU!

PORPUS IS A BEAST! PASS IT ON!

WHAT'S THE MATTER WITH THEM?

NO IDEA. LOCK THEM UP DOWN BELOW!

PORTER, WE WANT TO SEE OUR FRIEND CACOFONIX THE BARD

I'M NOT A PORTER AND YOU CAN'T!

VERY WELL THEN, WE SHALL TEAR OUT THESE BARS ONE BY ONE UNTIL YOU CO-OPERATE!

GO AHEAD AND TRY!

PLINNNK!

PLONNNK!

PLUNNNK!

STOP! LEAVE THE FIXTURES ALONE!

AH, ABOUT TIME TOO! WHAT SERVICE!

A HUGE CROWD IS FORMING OUTSIDE THE CIRCUS...

WASH YOUR TOGAS IN *SUPER PERSIC*! *SUPER PERSIC* WASHES EVEN PURPLER!

SCORE CARD! SCORE CARD!

CUSHIONS! CUSHIONS!

CHIPOLATAE! CANES CALIDI! CHIPOLATAE!

AND INSIDE THE IMPOSING ARENA THE TRUMPETS ANNOUNCE THE ARRIVAL OF CAESAR IN THE IMPERIAL BOX...

TANTAN TARA!!!!

PANEM ET CIRCENSES

LONG LIVE CAESAR!

CAESAR FOR EVER!

EVERYONE APPLAUDS THE DICTATOR...

CLAP! CLAP! CLAP! CLAP! CLAP! CLAP!

CLAP! CLAPCLAP! CLAP! CLAP! CLAP! CLAP!

ET TU BRUTE!

CLAP! CLAP! CLAP!

CLAP! CLAP! CLAP! CLAP!

* YOU TOO, BRUTUS!

THAT BRUTUS...I CAN SEE I'M GOING TO HAVE TROUBLE WITH HIM *

CLAPCLAP! CLAPCLAP! CLAPCLAP! CLAPCLAP!

* AN EXAMINATION OF ACT III, SCENE 1 OF JULIUS CAESAR BY WILLIAM SHAKESPEARE WILL INDICATE THE PROPHETIC NATURE OF THIS REMARK

THIS WILL BE A GREAT SHOW, O CAESAR!

I HOPE SO, CAIUS FATUOUS. IF NOT, YOU'LL BE IN ON THE ACT

LET THE GAMES BEGIN!

GULP!

45

... AND FINALLY I ASK YOU TO FREE THE GLADIATORS. THEY'RE GIVING UP THEIR BLOODTHIRSTY JOB!

GRANTED, O GAUL!

MMPH? IS THE SHOW OVER YET?

I ASK YOU TO FREE THE BARD WE CAME TO RESCUE, AND LET US GO HOME TO GAUL BEFORE WE HAVE TO BEAT YOUR ARMY UP AGAIN...

AND I HAVE ONE LAST FAVOUR TO ASK YOU, JULIUS...

YOU SAW THAT? NOT A BAD PROGRAMME, EH?

LEND US CAIUS FATUOUS THE GLADIATOR TRAINER FOR OUR JOURNEY BACK TO GAUL. WE'LL SEND HIM BACK BY RETURN

GRANTED, BY JUPITER!

BUT... BUT...

WHAT ARE YOU GOING TO DO WITH ME?

WE'RE GOING TO TEACH YOU A LITTLE LESSON, BY BELENOS!

LONG LIVE THE GAULS!

LONG LIVE THE GLADIATORS!

LONG LIVE CAESAR!

WHAT HAPPENED TO ME?

EXACTLY WHAT WILL HAPPEN AGAIN IF YOU DARE SING A NOTE BEFORE WE GET BACK TO GAUL!

NO FEAR! I'M NOT SINGING FOR ANY MORE ROMAN BARBARIANS, AND MOREOVER I'M TAKING NO FURTHER INTEREST IN THE MATTER!

HEY, WHERE ARE THE RUINS? DIDN'T A HOUSE FALL ON ME?

42

AND AFTER A FEW HOURS' WALK...

O EKONOMIKRISIS, PHOENICIAN MERCHANT, WILL YOU KEEP YOUR PROMISE AND TAKE US BACK TO GAUL?

MY OLD FRIENDS THE GAULS!!!

COME ABOARD, FRIENDS! BUSINESS WAS GOOD. I HAVE SOLD EVERYTHING, AND NOW I HAVE TO STOCK UP AGAIN!

WHO'S THIS?

A LITTLE SURPRISE FOR YOUR ROWING PARTNERS!

DO I... DO I HAVE TO ROW ALL BY MYSELF? ALL THE WAY BACK TO GAUL?

THIS WILL TEACH YOU TO DO A DIRTY JOB AND LIVE OFF OTHER PEOPLE'S MUSCLE!

WHY DON'T I SING A LITTLE SOMETHING TO LIVEN HIM UP?

NOOOO!

HE'S GREAT!

WHAT AN OARSMAN!

HEAR, HEAR!

SPLAT, SPLAT, SPAT, SPLAT, SPLAT, SPLAT

I FEEL WE MIGHT MAKE THIS ROMAN A PARTNER!

AN EXCELLENT NOTION, MR. CHAIRMAN!

BAH!

THE VOYAGE IS UNEVENTFUL, EXCEPT FOR A SKIRMISH WITH THE PIRATES...

CHEER UP, CAP'IN! WE'RE ALL IN THE SAME BOAT!

43

the end

ASTERIX
THE LEGIONARY

TEXT BY GOSCINNY

DRAWINGS BY UDERZO

TRANSLATED BY ANTHEA BELL AND DEREK HOCKRIDGE

The year is 50 BC. Gaul is entirely occupied by the Romans. Well, not entirely… One small village of indomitable Gauls still holds out against the invaders. And life is not easy for the Roman legionaries who garrison the fortified camps of Totorum, Aquarium, Laudanum and Compendium…

a few of the Gauls

Asterix, the hero of these adventures. A shrewd, cunning little warrior; all perilous missions are immediately entrusted to him. Asterix gets his superhuman strength from the magic potion brewed by the druid Getafix…

Obelix, Asterix's inseparable friend. A menhir delivery-man by trade; addicted to wild boar. Obelix is always ready to drop everything and go off on a new adventure with Asterix – so long as there's wild boar to eat, and plenty of fighting.

Getafix, the venerable village druid. Gathers mistletoe and brews magic potions. His speciality is the potion which gives the drinker superhuman strength. But Getafix also has other recipes up his sleeve…

Cacofonix, the bard. Opinion is divided as to his musical gifts. Cacofonix thinks he's a genius. Everyone else thinks he's unspeakable. But so long as he doesn't speak, let alone sing, everybody likes him…

Finally, Vitalstatistix, the chief of the tribe. Majestic, brave and hot-tempered, the old warrior is respected by his men and feared by his enemies. Vitalstatistix himself has only one fear; he is afraid the sky may fall on his head tomorrow. But as he always says, 'Tomorrow never comes.'

7

SNIFF

THIS IS ODD, O VITALSTATISTIX. WHY HAVE THE ROMANS TAKEN TO RECRUITING GAULS?

HUH!

JULIUS CAESAR'S IN TROUBLE IN AFRICA. HE'S OUT THERE FIGHTING THE ROMANS WHO SUPPORT POMPEY...

ACCORDING TO THE LATEST NEWS, HE'S BESIEGED IN RUSPINA *. HE NEEDS REINFORCEMENTS. HIS RECRUITING OFFICERS GO AROUND ASKING FOR VOLUNTEERS, AND WHEN THEY DON'T GET THEM THEY TAKE THEM BY FORCE...

*MONASTIR (TUNISIA)

WE'LL GO TO CONDATUM AT ONCE TO TRY AND GET YOUNG TRAGICOMIX BACK BEFORE HE LEAVES FOR AFRICA!

THAT'S EXACTLY WHAT I THOUGHT YOU'D SAY! IT JUST SHOWS YOUR INDOMITABLE COURAGE! PANACEA'S FIANCÉ...

BOOHOOHOOO!

PREPARATIONS FOR THE JOURNEY ARE QUICKLY MADE...

HERE'S SOME MAGIC POTION FOR YOU, ASTERIX

THANKS, O DRUID GETAFIX!

SNIFF!

...AND IT IS TIME TO LEAVE

HOW CAN I EVER THANK YOU?

YOU CAN THANK US WHEN WE BRING TRAGICOMIX BACK – AND BRING HIM BACK WE WILL, UNLESS THE SKY FALLS ON OUR HEADS!

BE A GOOD LITTLE DOG, DOGMATIX, I'LL BE BACK SOON...

I'D LIKE YOU TO LOOK AFTER DOGMATIX, PANACEA

I'LL TAKE CARE OF HIM, OBELIX...ISN'T HE SWEET!

GRRRR!

SMACK!

13

I'M RIGHT IN THE MIDDLE OF CARVING OUT THE LIST OF VOLUNTEER RECRUITS TO BE ISSUED TO ALL DEPARTMENTS... THERE HAVE TO BE TWELVE COPIES. WHAT WAS THE NAME AGAIN?

TRAGICOMIX

TRAGICOMIX... WITH A "T", AS IN TIMEO DANAOS ET DONA FERENTES?

AH, HERE WE ARE...TRAGICOMIX HAS LEFT WITH A CONVOY. AT THIS MOMENT HE'S DUE TO TAKE SHIP AT MASSILIA WITH REINFORCEMENTS FOR CAESAR. THEY'RE OFF TO AFRICA

AFRICA... HMMM...

OBELIX! COME HERE!

IS THAT YOU, ASTERIX?

YES!

COMING!

NOW THEN! LET'S BE POLITE!

WHAM!

?!!

TRAGICOMIX HAS LEFT FOR AFRICA. THE ONLY WAY TO GET HIM BACK NOW IS TO JOIN THE ROMAN ARMY

WHAT, US? JOIN THE ROMAN ARMY? STILL, IF YOU THINK IT WOULD HELP PANACEA..

SOON AFTERWARDS...

OUCH... WHAT DID THOSE TWO HAVE AGAINST ME, ANYWAY...?

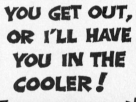

RIGHT! YOU'VE BEEN ASSIGNED TO THE 1ST LEGION, 3RD COHORT, 2ND MANIPLE, 1ST CENTURY. YOU HAVE TO REPEAT THAT WHEN PRESENTING YOURSELVES TO A SUPERIOR OFFICER!

THAT COOK IS CRAZY!

DID YOU REALLY ENJOY YOUR LUNCH?

YES, RATHER!

YOU, SHORTIE! PRESENT YOURSELF!

WHAT?

OH... ASTERIX THE GAUL!

AND I'M OBELIX! THE OTHERS ARE OUR PALS. WHAT'S YOUR NAME?

INSTRUCTOR DUBIUS STATUS, 1ST LEGION, 3RD COHORT...

GRRR... GET BACK INTO LINE, WILL YOU... GRR... GET BACK!

NOW WE DO PILUM DRILL. YOU TRY TO HIT THAT TARGET AT THE OTHER SIDE OF THE SQUARE, YOU START, LEGIONARY OBELIX

RIGHT!

TCHOC!

COOKHOUSE

ALL RIGHT, ALL RIGHT, ALL RIGHT! JUST GIVE ME TIME TO COOK THE BOARS, WILL YOU?

27

THE COLUMN OF THE 1ST LEGION, 3RD COHORT, 2ND MANIPLE, 1ST CENTURY IS STILL ON THE GO, BUT HAS UNDERGONE A SLIGHT MODIFICATION AS TO MARCHING ORDER...

HALT! WE'LL CAMP HERE FOR TONIGHT!

ER...UM...RIGHT! DIG A DITCH ROUND THE SITE... BUILD A STOCKADE! PITCH YOUR TENTS AROUND YOUR CENTURION'S TENT! ORGANISE SENTRY DUTY...

I SHOULDN'T BOTHER. LOOK AT 'EM!

!!! TONIGHT'S MENU: BOAR ON THE SPIT AND GÂTEAU À LA CRÈME

SUITS ME!

I'LL HAVE MY BOAR MEDIUM RARE, PLEASE

WHILE THEIR MEN ARE STUFFING THEMSELVES, THE TWO ROMAN OFFICERS MAKE DO WITH THE FRUGAL REGULATION MEAL IN THEIR SMALL REGULATION TENT...

HONK! SCRONTCH! SLOP!SLIP! SCRITCH MIAM!

AFTER A SHORT NIGHT'S SLEEP...

YAWN!

?

NEFARIUS PURPUS! THEY'VE GONE!

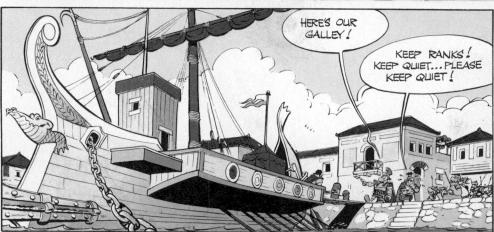

*ANCIENT GAULISH ARTIST

ASTERIX AND THE BIG FIGHT

TEXT BY GOSCINNY

DRAWINGS BY UDERZO

TRANSLATED BY ANTHEA BELL AND DEREK HOCKRIDGE

Asterix and the Big Fight

GAULISH VILLAGE

COMPENDIUM

LAUDANUM

AQUARIUM

TOTORUM

ARMORICA

BELGICA

LUTETIA

SPQR

GAUL
(ROMAN CONQUEST)
50 B.C.

CELTICA

PROVINCIA

AQUITANIA

The year is 50 BC. Gaul is entirely occupied by the Romans.
Well, not entirely... One small village of indomitable Gauls still
holds out against the invaders. And life is not easy for the
Roman legionaries who garrison the fortified camps of
Totorum, Aquarium, Laudanum and Compendium...

a few of the Gauls

Asterix, the hero of these adventures. A shrewd, cunning little warrior; all perilous missions are immediately entrusted to him. Asterix gets his superhuman strength from the magic potion brewed by the druid Getafix...

Obelix, Asterix's inseparable friend. A menhir delivery-man by trade; addicted to wild boar. Obelix is always ready to drop everything and go off on a new adventure with Asterix — so long as there's wild boar to eat, and plenty of fighting.

Getafix, the venerable village druid. Gathers mistletoe and brews magic potions. His speciality is the potion which gives the drinker superhuman strength. But Getafix also has other recipes up his sleeve...

Cacofonix, the bard. Opinion is divided as to his musical gifts. Cacofonix thinks he's a genius. Everyone else thinks he's unspeakable. But so long as he doesn't speak, let alone sing, everybody likes him...

Finally, Vitalstatistix, the chief of the tribe. Majestic, brave and hot-tempered, the old warrior is respected by his men and feared by his enemies. Vitalstatistix himself has only one fear; he is afraid the sky may fall on his head tomorrow. But as he always says, 'Tomorrow never comes.'

FIRST, THOSE WHO ACCEPTED THE PAX ROMANA AND WERE TRYING TO ADAPT TO THE POWERFUL CIVILISATION OF THE INVADERS...

WHAT ARE THESE PILLARS FOR?

THEY MAKE THE HOUSE LOOK GALLO-ROMAN

IF YOU ASK ME, IT LOOKS MORE GALLO-GREEK...

WHAT A GALL!

HE'S ALWAYS BEEN THAT WAY... IT'S VERY GALLING!

AND THEN THERE WERE THE OTHER GAULS, INDOMITABLE, BRAVE AND TOUGH, WHO LIKED THEIR FOOD AND DRINK, A GOOD FIGHT AND A BIT OF FUN, THE FINEST SPECIMENS BEING FOUND IN A SMALL TRIBE ALREADY KNOWN TO US...

HEY, HERE ARE ASTERIX AND OBELIX BACK FROM HUNTING!

WELL, BOYS, ANY NEWS?

NO. WE GOT A BOAR EACH

BUT I HAD DOGMATIX TO HELP ME. HE'S A GREAT BOARHOUND!!!

OH YES, I FORGOT... WE MET A ROMAN PATROL

THESE ROMANS ARE CRAZY!

5

MEANWHILE, IN THE FORTIFIED ROMAN CAMP OF TOTORUM...

THE...THE PATROL'S BACK, O CENTURION NEBULUS NIMBUS

BY JUPITER!!! WHAT HAPPENED TO **YOU?**

ER...WE MET A COUPLE OF GAULS...

AND THEY **DID** HAVE A DOG WITH THEM...

AND TWO BOARS!

SO THAT MADE FIVE!

THESE GAULS KEEP ON MAKING FOOLS OF US!

WE HAVE TO FIND A SOLUTION, O NEBULUS NIMBUS...IF THEY GET TO HEAR OF THIS IN ROME, YOU'LL BE UNDER A CLOUD!

SO WHAT DO YOU SUGGEST, O FELONIUS CAUCUS, MY RIGHT-HAND MAN?

WELL...

I'VE BEEN STATIONED IN THIS COUNTRY A LONG TIME. I KNOW THE GAULISH CUSTOMS. AND THERE'S ONE CUSTOM THAT MIGHT COME IN VERY USEFUL... IT'S CALLED **THE BIG FIGHT**

THE BIG FIGHT?

YES...WHEN THE CHIEF OF A GAULISH TRIBE WANTS TO BECOME THE CHIEF OF TWO GAULISH TRIBES, HE CHALLENGES ANOTHER CHIEF TO SINGLE COMBAT. THE LOSER AND HIS WHOLE TRIBE SUBMIT TO THE WINNER...

...IF BOTH CHIEFS ARE EQUALLY STRONG, THEY HAVE THE RIGHT TO THROW BALES OF STRAW AT EACH OTHER. THUS THE RESULT IS SAID TO BE DECIDED BY A STRAW VOTE...IF WE HAD A CHIEF WHO SUPPORTED US IN COMMAND OF THOSE INDOMITABLE GAULS, THERE'D BE NO PROBLEM...

BONK!

BIFF!

ALL RIGHT, BUT WHAT CHIEF WOULD BE CRAZY ENOUGH TO CHALLENGE THE TERRIBLE VITALSTATISTIX? HIS DRUID'S MAGIC POTION MAKES HIM INVINCIBLE!

I KNOW JUST THE MAN. HE'S A COLLABORATOR, AND AS COLOSSAL AS THE COLOSSEUM!

HERE COMES THE PATROL!

AHA!

MISSION ACCOMPLISHED. WE GOT THE DRUID!

WITH A PILUM?

ER...NO... WITH A MENHIR...

...AND WE LEFT HIM UNDER THE MENHIR. NO HUMAN BEING COULD SURVIVE A BLOW LIKE THAT!

I HOPE YOU'RE RIGHT...BUT I SOMETIMES WONDER IF THOSE GAULS ARE HUMAN...ANYWAY, WE'LL LET CASSIUS CERAMIX KNOW HE CAN COME AND CHALLENGE VITALSTATISTIX!

MEANWHILE...

ALL THE SAME, A LITTLE TAP WITH A MENHIR COULDN'T HAVE DONE HIM ANY HARM...MAYBE HE ATE SOMETHING HEAVY FOR LUNCH...

WE'RE COMING TO THE VILLAGE... I'M GOING TO TRY AND REVIVE HIM!

JUST A LITTLE TAP ON THE HEAD WITH A MENHIR...NOTHING TO SPEAK OF...

DONE IT! HE'S COMING BACK TO HIS SENSES! HE'S VERY STRONG, OUR DRUID, ESPECIALLY IN THE HEAD

HOW ARE YOU FEELING?

VERY WELL, THANK YOU...AND WHO MIGHT YOU BE, MY DEAR SIR?

IN THE FORTIFIED CAMP OF TOTORUM...

YOU TOLD ME GETAFIX THE DRUID HAD BEEN DISPOSED OF! NOT ONLY HAS HE NOT BEEN DISPOSED OF, HE'S IN A VERY GOOD MOOD! HE CAN'T STOP LAUGHING!

I'VE CHALLENGED VITALSTATISTIX, AND NOW I CAN'T WITHDRAW WITHOUT SUBMITTING TO HIM. I'M NOT SURE I WON'T, RATHER THAN GET MYSELF MURDERED...

THANKS VERY MUCH FOR YOUR ADVICE, FELONIUS CAUCUS! SO NOW I LOOK LIKE HAVING TWO REBEL VILLAGES ON MY HANDS INSTEAD OF ONE! OH, WON'T CAESAR BE PLEASED!

DON'T LET'S GET UPSET. WE STILL HAVE PLENTY OF TIME TO SEND PATROLS OUT TO THE FOREST TO CAPTURE THE DRUID...

QUOD ERAT DEMONSTRANDUM

OH, QUITE EASILY DONE!

MEANWHILE, IN THE GAULISH VILLAGE...

GETAFIX, YOU MUST LISTEN TO ME! YOU HAVE TO PREPARE THE MAGIC POTION TO GIVE OUR CHIEF SUPERHUMAN STRENGTH!

LOOK, WHO IS THIS GETAFIX YOU KEEP ON ABOUT?

LET'S GET EVERYTHING READY. PERHAPS HIS MEMORY WILL COME BACK. OBELIX, YOU GO AND FETCH THE INGREDIENTS FROM GETAFIX'S HUT, AND A CAULDRON

WOOAHAHAHA!

THAT FAT MAN IS PRICELESS!

ASTERIX, IF YOU DON'T TELL HIM TO STOP, DRUID OR NO DRUID, I SHALL TAKE THIS CAULDRON AND I'LL...

YOU'VE ALREADY DONE THAT WITH A MENHIR, OBELIX!

DAWN HAS NOT YET CRACKED WHEN...

ZZZ! ZZZ!

?

ON YOUR FEET, CHIEF! WE'LL START YOUR TRAINING WITH A BIT OF RUNNING!

COMING, ASTERIX!

COCKADOODLEDOO!

ONE, TWO, ONE, TWO! COME ON, BOYS, PUT SOME BEEF INTO IT, BY TOUTATIS!

?

NO, NO...THAT'S NOT THE WAY, VITALSTATISTIX! LET ME SHOW YOU!

THAT'S BETTER

MUCH BETTER

VERY MUCH BETTER

HM! HE'S NOT BEEFING SO MUCH NOW!

NOW YOU MUST HAVE SOME FIGHT TRAINING. YOU NEED A SPARRING PARTNER...

PUFF! PUFF! PUFF!

I CAN DO THAT JOB...

I'M NOT SURE WHETHER...

HE'S RIGHT. OBELIX IS IDEAL FOR THE PART. I SHAN'T BE AFRAID OF HURTING HIM

VERY WELL, LET'S STAR...

TCHONK!

BRAVO! OH, VERY CLEVER, OBELIX! WHEN YOU'RE AROUND THERE'S NO NEED FOR ANY ROMANS IN GAUL!!!

I WAS ONLY TRYING TO HELP...

32

36

WHILE THE COMBATANTS ARE IN TRAINING, THE ROMANS BUILD THE RING FOR THE BIG FIGHT OUTSIDE THE CAMP...

AND AS THE FIGHT AROUSES A GREAT DEAL OF PUBLIC INTEREST, NOMADIC BARBARIANS PUT UP THEIR SIDESHOWS NEARBY...

LIQUORIX BOARS

1 SESTERTIUS

DODGEM CHARIOTS

1ˢ

SHOOTING RANGE
5 BULL'S-EYES WINS A JAR OF BULL'S-EYES

CATAPULTS: 1 BRONZE COIN A SHOT
SPEARS: 2 BRONZE COINS A THROW

SWITCHBAX

THE GREAT DAY DAWNS AT LAST, AND A VAST CROWD ASSEMBLES, THEIR SHOUTS AND LAUGHTER MINGLING WITH THE SMELL OF BOAR AND CHIPS...

CHILDREN'S COMIX! 3 BRONZE COINS THE SLAB!

A GOLD COIN FOR ANYONE GOING ONE ROUND WITH THE MIRMILLO!

GET YOUR SOUVENIR MENHIRS HERE!

WILL THE PARENTS OF LITTLE ICELOLLIX PLEASE COME TO COLLECT HIM AT THE LOST CHILDREN'S TENT?

A PRESENT FROM THE ARMORICA FUN FAIR

LOST C

MENAGERIX SEE THE FABULOUS ANIMALS

W.H.Smix

BOUM!

38

GARRISON...SHOULDER ...ARMS! TO THE RINGSIDE...FORWARD ...MARCH!

HEY, INFIRMOFPURPUS, I WONDER IF YOUR OWL WON'T END UP BRINGING US BAD LUCK?

HE'S NOT *MY* OWL, AND IT'S NOT MY FAULT IF HE KEEPS FOLLOWING ME!

TO-WHIT, TO-WHOO!

CASSIUS CERAMIX ARRIVES AT THE RINGSIDE...

MEANWHILE...

O VITALSTATISTIX, IT'S TIME TO GO!

HEAVE AWAY, BOYS!

FRIENDS! I PROMISE TO DO MY UTMOST TO WIN, BY TOUTATIS!

LONG LIVE THE CHIEF!

I ONLY WANTED TO GIVE THEM A LITTLE SONG OF ENCOURAGEMENT...

OUR FRIENDS' VILLAGE IS ALMOST DESERTED...ONLY THE TWO DRUIDS ARE LEFT...

JUST TASTE THAT, MY DEAR SIR. I THINK YOU'LL BE AMUSED BY ITS PRESUMPTION!

I'VE MIXED A LITTLE SOMETHING MYSELF WHICH I THINK WILL SURPRISE YOU

... WITH OBELIX, A QUARRY TO REMORSE

OBELIX QUARRY

39

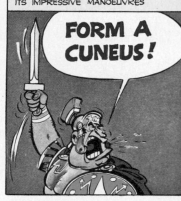

LONG LIVE VITALSTATISTIX! LONG LIVE GAUL!

ASTERIX AND THE CHIEFTAIN'S SHIELD

TEXT BY GOSCINNY

DRAWINGS BY UDERZO

TRANSLATED BY ANTHEA BELL AND DEREK HOCKRIDGE

Asterix and the Chieftain's Shield

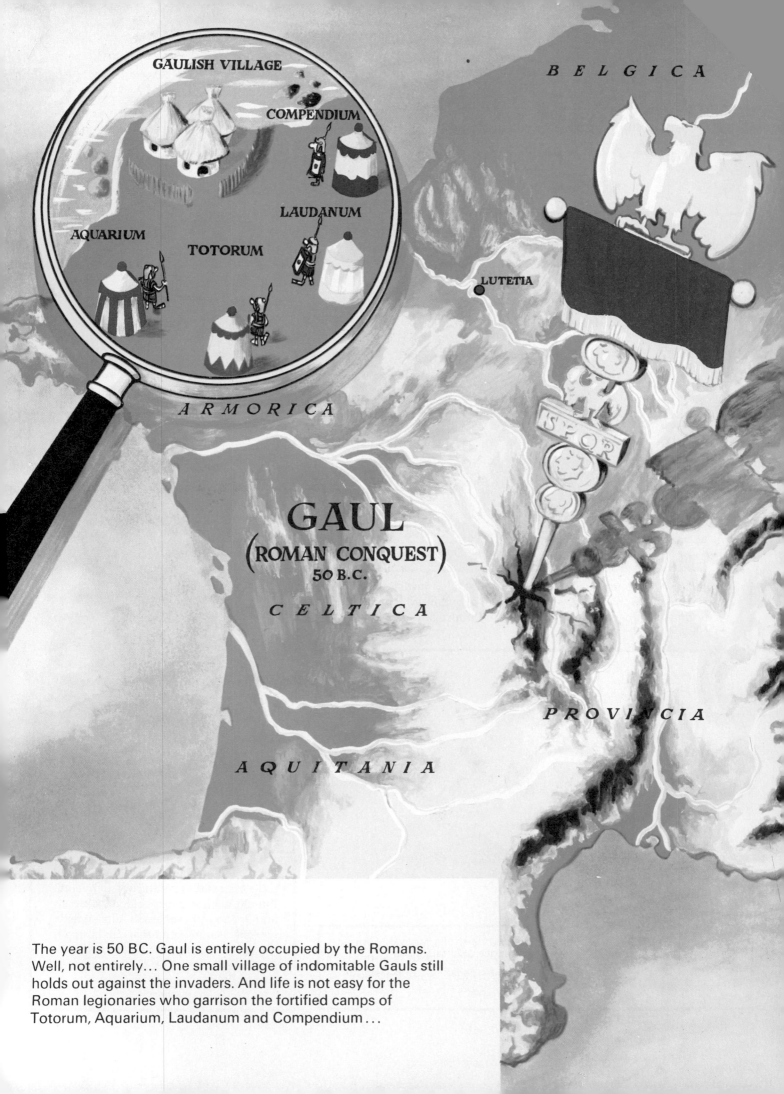

GAULISH VILLAGE

COMPENDIUM

LAUDANUM

AQUARIUM

TOTORUM

ARMORICA

BELGICA

LUTETIA

SPQR

GAUL
(ROMAN CONQUEST)
50 B.C.

CELTICA

PROVINCIA

AQUITANIA

The year is 50 BC. Gaul is entirely occupied by the Romans.
Well, not entirely... One small village of indomitable Gauls still
holds out against the invaders. And life is not easy for the
Roman legionaries who garrison the fortified camps of
Totorum, Aquarium, Laudanum and Compendium...

a few of the Gauls

Asterix, the hero of these adventures. A shrewd, cunning little warrior; all perilous missions are immediately entrusted to him. Asterix gets his superhuman strength from the magic potion brewed by the druid Getafix...

Obelix, Asterix's inseparable friend. A menhir delivery-man by trade; addicted to wild boar. Obelix is always ready to drop everything and go off on a new adventure with Asterix – so long as there's wild boar to eat, and plenty of fighting.

Getafix, the venerable village druid. Gathers mistletoe and brews magic potions. His speciality is the potion which gives the drinker superhuman strength. But Getafix also has other recipes up his sleeve...

Cacofonix, the bard. Opinion is divided as to his musical gifts. Cacofonix thinks he's a genius. Everyone else thinks he's un-speakable. But so long as he doesn't speak, let alone sing, everybody likes him...

Finally, Vitalstatistix, the chief of the tribe. Majestic, brave and hot-tempered, the old warrior is respected by his men and feared by his enemies. Vitalstatistix himself has only one fear; he is afraid the sky may fall on his head tomorrow. But as he always says, 'Tomorrow never comes.'

VERCINGETORIX, DEFEATED AT THE SIEGE OF ALESIA, THROWS HIS ARMS AT CAESAR'S FEET... AND OFFICIALLY, ALL GAUL IS CONQUERED...

OUCH!

AFTER THIS MELANCHOLY CEREMONY, CAESAR SETS OFF IN SEARCH OF FRESH CONQUESTS...

...AND THE ARMS OF THE ARVERNIAN CHIEFTAIN LIE WHERE THEY HAVE FALLEN. NO ONE DARES TOUCH THEM...

... UNTIL SUNSET, WHEN A ROMAN ARCHER SUCCUMBS TO TEMPTATION AND MAKES OFF WITH A MAGNIFICENT SHIELD...

HEY, HOW ABOUT A GAME OF RUBER ET NIGER?

... WHICH HE LOSES AT ONCE IN A GAME OF CHANCE.

DIEM PERDIDI!

YOU CAN QUOTE ME ON THAT TOO!

THE WINNER, A LEGIONARY OUT WITHOUT A PASS, FINDS THE PRESENT TENSE WHEN TRYING TO SNEAK INTO CAMP, HE IS PICKED UP BY A CENTURION WITH AN ACTIVE VOICE...

HEY, YOU THERE! QUO VADIS, LADDIE?

... AND IN AN IMPERATIVE MOOD, WHO CONFISCATES THE SHIELD IN RETURN FOR HIS SILENCE.

O TEMPORA! O MORES!

THE CENTURION, HAVING SPENT ALL HIS PAY, SWOPS THE PRECIOUS SHIELD FOR AN AMPHORA OF WINE AT A WINE AND CHARCOAL MERCHANT'S...

..., AND THE SHOPKEEPER SUBSEQUENTLY AGREES TO HAND IT OVER TO A GAULISH WARRIOR WHO HAS ESCAPED FROM ALESIA...

... AND IS TRYING TO DROWN HIS SORROWS IN DRINK ...

WELL, IF IT GIVES YOU ANY SATISFACTION...

HIC!

5

SO ALL GAUL IS OCCUPIED. ALL? NO! ONE LITTLE GAULISH VILLAGE IS STILL HOLDING OUT AGAINST THE INVADERS. A LITTLE VILLAGE WE KNOW VERY WELL, WHERE MORALE IS HIGH, AND ANY EXCUSE WILL DO TO HOLD A BANQUET WITH LOTS TO EAT AND DRINK. AS IT HAPPENS, THE LAST SUCH BANQUET HAS HAD SOME UNFORTUNATE CONSEQUENCES...

OOOOW! OOOOOOH! OH! OH! OH!

IS SOMEONE SLAUGHTERING A WILD BOAR?

NO, IT'S OUR BARD SINGING A LULLABY!

MAKE WAY FOR THE DRUID! CHIEF VITALSTATISTIX IS ILL!

IT'S THE SAME OLD STORY: THE DAY AFTER HE'S BEEN EATING AND DRINKING AND MAKING MERRY WITH THOSE BARBARIANS HE FEELS AS IF THE SKY HAD FALLEN ON HIS HEAD!

IT ISN'T MY HEAD THAT HURTS!

DOES IT HURT THERE, THEN?

AH, YES, HE'S GOT LIVER TROUBLE.

I NEVER KNEW ANYONE COULD GET LIVER TROUBLE...

OUUCH!

I WISH I WAS DEAD!

YOUR WIFE IMPEDIMENTA IS RIGHT, O CHIEF, I'M AFRAID YOU ATE AND DRANK RATHER TOO MUCH AT OUR LAST BANQUET.

I NEVER KNEW ANYONE COULD EAT TOO MUCH.

I WOULDN'T MIND A HOLIDAY IN THOSE PARTS...

RIGHT, I'M GOING TO SEND YOU TO SEE THE DRUID DIAGNOSTIX, WHO RUNS THE FAMOUS HYDRO AT AQUAE CALIDAE.

AND WE'LL GO WITH YOU, O VITAL STATISTIX! A CHIEF OUGHT TO HAVE AN ESCORT!

YES, AND DOGMATIX CAN COME TOO! A SLIMMING CURE MIGHT DO HIM GOOD. HE'S GETTING FAT.

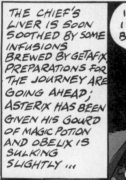

THE CHIEF'S LIVER IS SOON SOOTHED BY SOME INFUSIONS BREWED BY GETAFIX PREPARATIONS FOR THE JOURNEY ARE GOING AHEAD; ASTERIX HAS BEEN GIVEN HIS GOURD OF MAGIC POTION AND OBELIX IS SULKING SLIGHTLY...

I KNOW, I KNOW, I DON'T GET ANY BECAUSE GNGNGN GNGNGN...

I'M A BIT SORRY TO LEAVE THE VILLAGE, BUT WE CAN HAVE A GREAT BANQUET TO CELEBRATE OUR DEPARTURE AND...

BANQUET? I'M SICK AND TIRED OF SACRIFICING MYSELF FOR A GREAT FAT BARBARIAN WITHOUT THE GUMPTION OF A WILD BOAR PIGLET...

...WHO DOESN'T SHOW ME THE LEAST CONSIDERATION AFTER I'VE GIVEN HIM THE BEST YEARS OF MY L...

COME ON, BOYS, LET'S GO.

THEY'RE... THEY'RE GOING! WITHOUT TELLING ANYONE!

CACOFONIX! CACOFONIX!

THE CHIEF'S OFF, WITH ASTERIX AND OBELIX!

HMPH? WHAT?

QUICK! I WILL NOW GIVE THEM A SONG OF...

OH NO, YOU WON'T! OH NO, YOU WON'T!

GOT THE ITINERARY?

YES, ASTERIX, AND THIS SLAB LISTS ALL THE BEST INNS ALONG OUR WAY.

BUT AREN'T YOU SUPPOSED TO BE ON A DIET?

WELL, IF I'M GOING TO HAVE A COURSE OF TREATMENT I MIGHT AS WELL MAKE IT WORTH WHILE. ANYWAY, THAT'S ALL ROT; I FEEL FINE. I WAS SUFFERING FROM A SPOT OF MENTAL FATIGUE, THAT'S ALL.

THERE! I ALWAYS KNEW EATING COULDN'T MAKE ANYONE ILL!

...AND THE JOURNEY BECOMES A GASTRONOMIC TOUR, WITH BANQUET FOLLOWING BANQUET...

GOOD FOOD NEVER HURT ANYONE, MY LADS...

SCRUNCH!

SCRUNCH!

...PUNCTUATED BY THE WISE AND MORALLY ELEVATING MAXIMS OF VITALSTATISTIX...

...SO LONG AS YOU DON'T GO TOO HEAVY ON THE SAUCES.

... MANY OF THEM STILL CURRENT TODAY AMONG PEOPLE ON A STRICT DIET.

USE A LITTLE WINE FOR THY STOMACH'S SAKE!

5A

AND SO, IN DUE COURSE ...

LET GOOD DIGESTION WAIT ON APPETITE ...

SCRUNCH! SCRUNCH!

... OUR FRIENDS ARRIVE AT THE GATES OF AQUAE CALIDAE, THE END OF THEIR JOURNEY.

... AND CHEESE IS AN AID TO DIGESTION.

I'LL JUST HAVE A LITTLE NAP UNDER THAT TREE, BOYS. MY HEAD FEELS A BIT HEAVY ...

?!

NNNNNNNN

BL BL BL BL BL

OOOUUUUCH!

5B

9

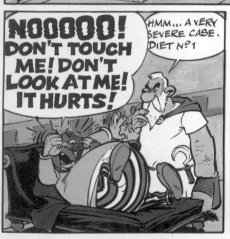

VITALSTATISTIX STARTS HIS TREATMENT. HE DRINKS THE WATER OF THE SPRINGS AT REGULAR INTERVALS...

... USES THE SOPHISTICATED MODERN SHOWER SYSTEM...

... AND STICKS TO A STRICT DIET BASED ON BOILED VEGETABLES.

AND THIS IS WHERE THE TROUBLE BEGINS, SINCE ASTERIX AND OBELIX, AS THE CHIEF'S ESCORT, HAVE PERMISSION TO SHARE HIS TABLE AT MEAL TIMES...

HEY THERE! ANOTHER BOAR!

SNAP!

AND MORE BEER!

SOME OF THE OTHER PATIENTS BEGIN TO CRACK UP...

BOO...BOOHOOOHOOO!

AND SERIOUS INCIDENTS ARE ONLY JUST AVERTED.

IF YOU GO TAKING ADVANTAGE OF HIM TO STEAL HIS BONE BECAUSE HE'S SO SMALL I SHALL POKE YOU IN THE LIVER WITH MY FINGER!

GRRRR!

THE TREATMENT INCLUDES BATHING IN WATER FROM THE HOT SPRINGS.

IS IT NICE?

HMPFF!

HEY, ASTERIX, I'D LIKE TO TAKE A DIVE!

OBELIX, NOOOO!

SPLOSH!

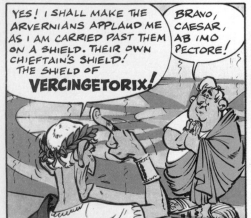

WELL, MY DEAR VAPUS, YOU'LL JUST HAVE TO GO BACK TO GAUL AND LOOK FOR THE SHIELD VERCINGETORIX THREW AT MY FEET.

ER ... CAESAR ... IT MIGHT SAVE TIME TO USE SOME OTHER SHIELD ... A NICE NEW ONE. I HAPPEN TO KNOW A LITTLE ARMOURER WHO ...

VADE RETRO, VAPUS! I SHALL HAVE MY TRIUMPH ON THAT ARVERNIAN SHIELD AND NONE OTHER! AND DON'T YOU TRY TO DECEIVE ME! TO DECEIVE CAESAR IS TO DECEIVE THE GODS, AND THE ANGER OF THE GODS WOULD BE TERRIBLE!

AND AS TRIBUNE NOXIUS VAPUS RELUCTANTLY SETS OFF FOR GAUL AGAIN, OUR HEROES ARE ENJOYING THEIR HOLIDAY ... THEY VISIT THE FAMOUS PUY DE DÔME (HERE SEEN LOOKING SOUTH. TO SEE IT LOOKING NORTH, TURN ROUND.)

... AND THE TEMPLE OF LUG, GOD OF BUSINESS AND INDUSTRY ...

OUR VERY OWN GOD!

... AND THE TOWNS OF NEMESSOS ①, NERIOMAGUS ② BORVO ③ AND CALENTES BAIAE ④

AND WHAT ABOUT ALESIA?

ALESIA?

① CLERMONT-FERRAND ② NERIS
③ LA BOURBOULE ④ CHAUDES-AIGUES

WHAT DO YOU MEAN, ALESIA, EH??? WHY BRING ALESIA INTO IT?

WE DON'T EVEN KNOW WHERE ALESIA IS, SO THERE!

AN ATTITUDE WHICH HAS PERSISTED DOWN THE CENTURIES, WITH THE RESULT THAT THE SCENE OF THE GAULS' DEFEAT BY CAESAR IS STILL UNKNOWN... A REGRETTABLY CHAUVINIST STATE OF AFFAIRS!

OUR FRIENDS RETURN TO GERGOVIA. EVERYONE KNOWS WHERE GERGOVIA IS.

YOU'LL STAY AT OUR PLACE AGAIN, WON'T YOU?

WITH PLEASURE, BUT WE'LL DO THE SHOPPING TODAY. HOW ABOUT SOME BOARS?

GOOD IDEA. WE'LL BRING HOME THE BACON.

DON'T BE RASHER THAN YOU MUST.

WE'RE NEVER HAM-HANDED!

I HOPE THAT'S NOT JUST GAMMON!

TAP TAP TAP TAP TAP!

19

VAPUS IS NOTORIOUS IN THESE PARTS. CAESAR SENDS HIM TO KEEP US DOWN. IF HE'S BACK, WE'RE IN FOR A BAD TIME!

OH, DON'T LET'S BOTHER ABOUT A LITTLE THING LIKE THAT!

IT'S A REAL PLEASURE TO COOK FOR A MAN WHO ENJOYS HIS FOOD!

OH, I SAY!

MEANWHILE, TRIBUNE NOXIUS VAPUS ARRIVES AT THE PREFECT'S PALACE...

?

AVE, NOXIUS VAPUS! I DIDN'T EXPECT YOU BACK SO SOON... ER... DID YOU HAVE A GOOD JOURNEY?

SUMMON ALL THE COMMANDING OFFICERS OF THE LOCAL GARRISONS AT ONCE. ALL LEAVE IS CANCELLED!

HEAR THAT? JOIN UP, THEY SAID. IT'S A MAN'S LIFE, THEY SAID...

SOON AFTERWARDS...

WELL, THOSE ARE YOUR ORDERS: FIND THE CHIEFTAIN'S SHIELD SO THAT CAESAR CAN HOLD HIS TRIUMPH IN GERGOVIA!

A LOT OF ALESIANS CAME TO LIVE IN GERGOVIA AFTER THEIR DEFEAT. THAT GIVES US A GOOD OPENING. SEARCH EVERY HOUSE! AND GET MOVING, BY JUPITER!

ANICIUM: LE PUY

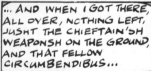

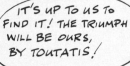

NOW THEN, DON'T FORGET TO LOOK ILL!

ALL RIGHT, ALL RIGHT, DON'T GO ON ABOUT IT! I GET THE IDEA!

KNOCK KNOCK KNOCK!

DAVID THERAPEVTIX DIRECTOR

GOOD MORNING, GENTLEMEN.

GOOD MORNING, O DRUID.

OUCH.

DAVID THERAPEVTIX DIRECTOR

WHAT SEEMS TO BE THE TROUBLE?

HE'S ILL. I'M ILL. EVEN OUR DOG IS ILL. WE WANT THE FULL TREATMENT!

LET'S SEE... DOES IT HURT THERE?

OUCH.

AND THERE?

OUCH.

WELL, THAT'S CLEAR! LET'S SAY BATHS AND SHOWERS, MASSAGE AND SAUNAS...

OUCH.

...AND OF COURSE A STRICT DIET.

OUCH!

RIGHT, THE FULL TREATMENT FOR BOTH OF YOU. NOT THE DOG, THOUGH. THE SCIENCE OF HYDROTHERAPY IS STILL IN ITS INFANCY, AND WE DON'T KNOW IF IT'S GOOD FOR ANIMALS.

AND SO, IN THE COURSE OF TREATMENT, OUR FRIENDS ARE ABLE TO MAKE DISCREET ENQUIRIES...

WHAT'S YOUR NAME?

APPLEJUS

CARROTJUS.

PRUNEJUS.

TOMATOJUS.

THE TREATMENT IS PARTICULARLY PAINFUL AT MEALTIMES...

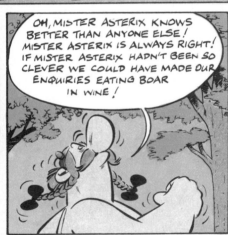

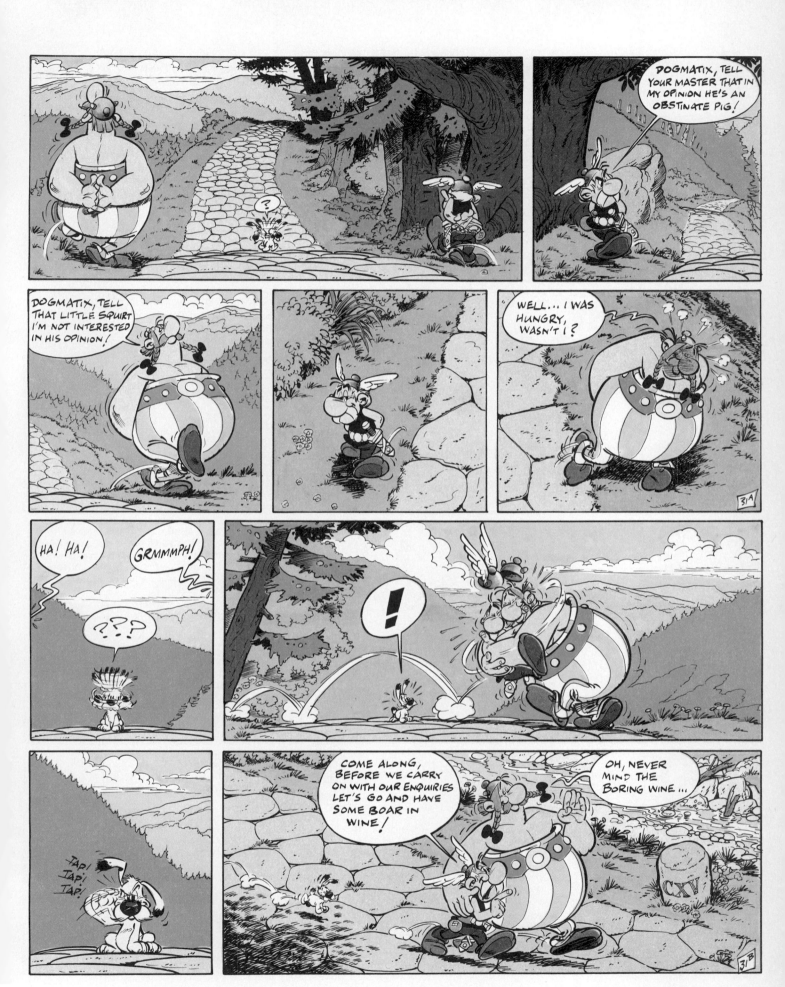

35

LATER, AFTER BORROWING A ROMAN CHARIOT WHICH WAS JUST PASSING...

WE MUST GET TO GERGOVIA BEFORE CRAPULUS, TO STOP HIM GIVING THE SHIELD TO THE ROMANS...

IF HE GETS THERE FIRST WE'VE HAD IT. WE CAN'T FIGHT THE WHOLE GARRISON!

WHY NOT? IS IT OUT OF BOUNDS?

LATE THAT NIGHT...

WINES SPIRIX

WINES CHARCOAL

WHO... WHO'S THERE?

IT'S US! OBELIX, ASTERIX...

...AND DOGMATIX!

COME IN, QUICK! THE SKY HAS FALLEN ON OUR HEADS!

?!

AND THERE'S A PRICE ON YOURS, BY THE WAY... THE ROMANS HAVE GONE CRAZY! THEY'RE SEARCHING EVERYWHERE, AND THE WORST OF IT IS...

...MY WINESANSPIRIX HAS DISAPPEARED! NOXIUS VAPUS MUST HAVE TAKEN HIM PRISONER! BOO HOO HOO!

NEVER MIND THE SHIELD! WE'LL FIND YOUR WINESANSPIRIX, BY TOUTATIS!

YOU CAN BE BOUND WE WILL, EVEN IF THE GARRISON IS OUT OF BOUNDS, BY BELENOS!

SNIFF!

AND SO THE OUTLAWED ASTERIX, OBELIX (AND DOGMATIX) SPEND THE NIGHT HIDDEN IN A HEAP OF CHARCOAL...

GOOD NIGHT, OBELIX.

SORRY I LOST MY TEMPER EARLIER. YOU'RE A WHITE MAN, ASTERIX!

42

O ROMANS!

WHAT'S UP?

OH, NOTHING... DON'T TAKE ANY NOTICE...

TAKE A GOOD LOOK! AND YOU, BRAVE PEOPLE OF GERGOVIA, COME AND WATCH OUR TRIUMPH!

THE TRIUMPH OF CHIEF VITALSTATISTIX ON THE SHIELD OF VERCINGETORIX!

RIGHT. VENI, VIDI, AND I GET THE IDEA. NO ONE MUST EVER KNOW I SAW THIS... AND AS I CANNOT CONGRATULATE YOU ON THE CURIOUS APPEARANCE OF YOUR TROOPS...

... AND SO AS TO MAKE SURE MY VISIT REMAINS A SECRET, I'M SENDING YOU AND YOUR MEN TO A GARRISON IN NUMIDIA...

AH! AT LAST! TWO CLEAN SOLDIERS!

HIC!

HIC!

CENTURION! I PROMOTE YOU TO OFFICER COMMANDING THE GARRISON OF GERGOVIA! LEGIONARY, I PROMOTE YOU TO CENTURION! AND I NEVER WANT TO HEAR THE NAME OF THIS TOWN AGAIN! AVE!

AVE! DON'T YOU WORRY, WE'LL KEEP ON THE BEST OF TERMS WITH THE WINE MERCHANTS OF THESE PARTS, ME AND PUSILLANIMUS!

CENTURION PUSILLAN -HIC! - MUS!

47

OUR FRIENDS ARE QUITE SORRY TO LEAVE GERGOVIA AFTER THEIR MEMORABLE TRIUMPH...

ON THE WAY HOME THE CHIEF'S STATISTICS ARE REVITALIZED AS HE VISITS ALL THE INNS HE PATRONIZED ON THE OUTWARD JOURNEY.

OUR VILLAGE!

AND ONCE AGAIN OUR STORY ENDS WITH A BANQUET... EVERYONE IS THERE. EVERYONE? NO, SOMEONE IS MISSING... WHO CAN IT BE?

NOT HIM; HE'S THERE ALL RIGHT. SO WHO CAN IT BE, THEN?

...WHO?

BUT, IMPEDIMENTA, I HAVE TO SIT AT THE HEAD OF THE TABLE! I HAVE TO GO! I'M CURED, MY LOVE...

IMPEDIMENTA! YOU'RE NOT GOING TO HIT ME OVER THE HEAD WITH THAT SHIELD, ARE YOU ?!?

THE END